# FRONDES SALICIS

T0382353

# FRONDES SALICIS

BY

## A. B. RAMSAY

MASTER OF MAGDALENE COLLEGE
CAMBRIDGE

AUTHOR OF *INTER LILIA* AND
*ROS ROSARUM*

CAMBRIDGE
AT THE UNIVERSITY PRESS
1935

## CAMBRIDGE
### UNIVERSITY PRESS

University Printing House, Cambridge CB2 8BS, United Kingdom

Cambridge University Press is part of the University of Cambridge.

It furthers the University's mission by disseminating knowledge in the pursuit of education, learning and research at the highest international levels of excellence.

www.cambridge.org
Information on this title: www.cambridge.org/9781316603765

© Cambridge University Press 1935

First published 1935
First paperback edition 2015

*A catalogue record for this publication is available from the British Library*

ISBN 978-1-316-60376-5 Paperback

*Green and grey willow-leaves,*
  *Green and grey in one,*
*Whitening and shadowing*
  *In wind and sun:*
*Emblem of youth and age*
  *On the same ground*
*By golden Fortune*
  *In friendship found:*

*Chaplet of willow-leaves*
  *For Age I twine,*
*Age that befriended*
  *When youth was mine:*
*Chaplet of willow-leaves*
  *I bind on the brow*
*Of Youth delightful*
  *In friendship now.*

## TWO RIVERS

Tamesis et Camus iucundo flumine rident;
  deliciis animum captat uterque suis.
Non hic est illo, non hoc est carior ille,
  sed nobis ambo consecrat unus amor.

## ACROSTIC

HIC ego si fuero, sim forsitan ILLE futurus.

1    Hoc, si vis pacem, patria nostra, para.

2  Qui me dant operi pueros laudate, magistri.

3    Tu dare tum nonvis cum tibi nummus adest.

4  Si languent taedae, lentis hoc addite flammis.

5    Adde caput caudae: cauda fit umbra mihi.

6  Aspice, pars toti par est, mirabile visu.

7    Etsi me vertes, vix ego versus ero.

8  Nunc invertendo vinces, invertere iussus.

9    In Syrtes curo ne tua navis eat.

BONVS PVER : MAGNVS VIR

bellum, opera, neg-as, unguen, sciuru-s,
  pars, usrev, etrevni, rector.

## THE DESCENT OF MAN

Relliquias operis, scissae fragmenta papyri,
    cur ita per sellas spargis, inepte puer?
Hoc faciunt parvi lascivo dente catelli
    cum plumas vellunt dilaniantque pilas.
Sic lignum gaudet damnoso perdere rostro
    psittacus et caveae strage replere solum.
Talibus indiciis 'hominum' Darvinius ille
    'progenitor' dixit 'cercopithecus erat'.


## ATTRACTION

Omnia quae vivunt ducit nonnulla voluptas;
    gallus amat stercus; flumina quaerit anas.
Vertitur ad solem solis flos; sepia sensim
    Caecilii digitos ad sua vasa trahit.
Nec puerum culpo; vix conscius esse videtur,
    et capit ignarum proximitate liquor.
Paret naturae, labens ut ab arbore malum
    ad terram trahitur nec sine lege cadit.

## 3

### ACROSTIC

HINC stat Maeonides, ILLINC armatus Achilles;
    hic nobis vivit quod vetat ille mori.
Arma ducum pereunt; contemnunt carmina mortem.
    Dixerunt veteres 'plus stilus ense potest'.

1 Vergilius 'possunt' dixit 'quia posse videntur';
    si quis me voluit dicere, magna potest.

2 Si mihi, docte puer, sanctam subieceris urbem,
    sidereo fiam magnus in axe gigas.

3 Conveniens mediae vox est Hebraica brumae,
    tempore nobiscum quo Deus esse solet.

4 Si, puer, argento credis pretiosius aurum,
    parce meos monitus temnere, parce loqui.

5 Dux ovium venio, saevo tamen ore cavendus;
    moenia, si pepuli, collabefacta ruunt.

POETA: MILES

possum, Ori-on, Emmanuel, tace, aries.


## TWINKLE, TWINKLE, LITTLE STAR; NOW WE ALL KNOW WHAT YOU ARE

O parva summo stella micans polo,
quae corda caeca nuper origine
    humana turbabas, ab ipsis
      astrologis meliora docti

nunc scimus omnes corpore quo tua
natura constet, cassitero calens
    fumante ventosisque nitri
      nubibus hydrogenaque vivo.

## WISE AFTER THE EVENT

Praescius es rerum, Fronto, sed inutilis idem;
  tum cum praeteriit dicis adesse malum.
'Id te facturum' cantas 'si forte putassem,
  id ne tu faceres praemoniturus eram.'
Crastina quin potius curas? Hesterna fuerunt.
  Posse frui vita, non potuisse volo.


## A ROYAL VISIT

En, subeunt Aedem rex et regina Minorem.
  Stamus, honorati conscia turba loci.
Officii memores habitum mutamus inertem
  corporis, et tacitos cogimus esse pedes.
Erigimus frontem; toto reverentia voltu
  fixa sedet, bracis exserimusque manus.
Incedunt pueri regali veste choristae,
  et non indocto tollimus ore modos.
Rex semel aspiciens monstrat quo more gerendi
  sint semper ritus aspiciente Deo.

## DRAWN MATCHES

Quattuor hos annos nobis Harrovia certat:
  victrix e bello neutra caterva redit.
Haec ingrata mora est. Nimium, Victoria, dormis.
  Surge; sed a nostra surgere parte velis.


## HE FOLLOWS HIS NOSE

Semper in obliquum noster se Fimbria vertit;
  et, cur id faciat, Lentule, causa patet.
Nam sequitur quoquo coepit praecedere nasus,
  qui misero prava stat regione viro.


## VALE

Nunc iterum dulces campos flumenque relinquo
  nunc iterum dico 'dulcis Etona, vale'.
Hic laetus didicique puer docuique magister;
  bis facilis durum Musa fefellit opus.
Hic multos inter risus rarumque dolorem,
  quae puero fuerat, sors fuit illa viro.
Nunc repetens primae felicia regna iuventae
  respicio laetos prospicioque dies.

## VALETE

Quarta, vale, Classis. Pueri, mea turba, valete.
  Si peccatis adhuc, non mea culpa fuit.
Saepe malum vobis correxit tessera morem,
  saepe timor ferulae, saepe pudendus apex.
Corripuit vacuam mentem vox dira magistri;
  postpositae tergo corripuere manus.
Si quis adhuc vestrum puer est informis et horrens—
  quod poteram feci; non mea culpa fuit.


## COMMON SENSE

Quinque deus nobis sensus dedit, unde solemus
  perpetua rerum cognitione frui.
Caeruleum video caelum camposque virentes,
  et volucrum patula cantus in aure sonat.
Nonne placent naso flores, et mella palato?
  nonne potest quidvis tangere certa manus?
Sic externa patet species naturaque rerum,
  vitaque per quinas gaudet inire fores.
Sed sine Mente Bona tot tantaque gaudia sordent,
  et patior brutae quod patiuntur oves.
Mulus et anser habent quot sunt in corpore sensus;
  Mens Bona, tu mecum semper amanda veni.
Sic varios inter comites acceptior ibo;
  sic discam summo gratior esse deo.

## ABSENT THOUGHTS

Si sapis, absentem, Muraena, recollige mentem.
    (Ite Leonini, fortiter ite, modi.)
Num similem lasso vitam vis ducere Crasso,
    qui nescit factis totus adesse suis?
Ille——nec est rarum——currens per strata viarum
    irruit in populum, fitque ruina senum.
Spargere narratur, dum mens incerta vagatur,
    sacchara per carnem, per melimela salem.
Nuper iucundas sese mersurus in undas
    iverat ad ripam, care Cuculle, tuam.
Qualibus haec verbis referam? Se stravit in herbis
    iactis flumineas vestibus inter aquas.
Tu tibi sis custos; mores nanciscere iustos,
    et menti rigidas, si volat, adde seras.
Adde seras menti; properat sub imagine venti,
    interdumque fugit nec revocata redit.
Ite, Leonini versus; accurrite fini.
    Finis adest: nostros Musa coronat equos.


## EX ORE INFANTIUM

Omnibus in terris, Deus, admirabile nomen
    est Tibi, cui magno stat super axe decus.
En, ego perficio laudem Tibi nescius infans.
    Sic pereunt hostes; vis inimica silet.
Suspicio lunam diversaque sidera caeli,
    compositum digitis grande creantis opus;
'Quid sumus?' inquiro; 'cur nos in mente tueris?'
    Caelicolis minor est, cetera magnus homo.
Squamigerum regit ille genus variasque volucres
    et tardas pecudes praecipitesque feras.

## DAVID

Electe fratres ante tuos puer,
ex ore laudans indocili Deum,
victor Palaestini gigantis,
auspice te pueri minores,

aetate prima quodquod inibimus
certamen, acri nec timida manu
nitemur, et saevos leones
et rabidas subigemus ursas.

## A WORD TO CAESAR

*from* SMITH *min.*

Saepe Faber minimus laudo te, maxime Caesar;
arte tua, fateor, non male bella geris.
Et tamen interdum nonnulla est causa querendi
cum calamum sumis gestaque bella refers.
Recte quod poteras, oblique dicere mavis,
et cumulas uno plurima verba loco.
Tunc opus est nobis, tunc est labor Hercule dignus,
tum medio lux est invenienda chao.
Turbatas acies componimus ordine certo;
solvimus ambages, et tua facta patent.
Vicimus ad finem, sed non sine vulnere multo.
Auxiliis grates, maxime Caesar, habe.

## TO OVID

Condere quo poteras, Ovidi, tot carmina pacto?
  Sic utinam possem iungere verba modis.
Dicere per numeros nil non potuisse videris;
  omnia verborum mobilitate facis.
Nil metuis; caecas feliciter inter arenas
  radit inoffensam tuta carina viam.
Monstra, deos, nymphas minimo conamine narras,
  quique volant homines, quaeque loquuntur aves.
Me virides herbas et dulcia rura canentem
  tristibus insidiis horrida culpa capit.
Me nemora aptantem numeris et fluminis undas
  Orbilius ferula corrigit ille senex.

## Μηδὲν ἄγαν

'Nil nimium facias' veteres cecinere poetae;
  'Nil nimium facias' saecula nostra canunt.
'Nil nimium', memini, nutrix annosa monebat;
  'Nil nimium' mater saepe paterque monent.
'Nil nimium', cantant duro sermone magistri,
  'Omnibus in rebus credimus esse modum.'
'Quod satis est, par est epulis' et talia dicunt,
  sive iubent vocem sistere sive gulam.
Ne nimium ludam, vigilat custodia circum;
  ne nimium cessem, sedula turba cavet.
Ne nimium discam, nemo trepidare videtur,
  neve meum rumpam cognitione caput.

## THE PICTURES

Tot sine fine movens rapidas cinema figuras
    scenarumque vices quam vehementer amo.
Naufragia aspicio, pugnas, incendia, caedes,
    et captos homines praecipitesque fugas.
Alta, velut feles, repunt per tecta latrones;
    ferrea nocturno rumpitur arca dolo.
Rivales coeunt, et amans occidit amantem;
    vi famuli pereunt et iugulantur heri.
Haec quoties narro, trepidat carissima mater
    ne vitient animum talia visa meum.
Sed pater 'assuescat iam nunc horroribus,' inquit,
    'quid sit vitandum sentiat inde puer'.

## THE BOAT RACE

Sunt duo non tardis illustria flumina remis;
    eximium nomen Camus et Isis habent.
Est mihi, confiteor, par non ignobile fratrum,
    nec sum certus utri sit tribuenda fides.
Stat minor a Camo, stat maior ab Iside frater;
    me vocat hinc maior, me vocat inde minor.
Quid minimus faciam? Sibi me devinxit uterque.
    Concolor ambobus scilicet esse velim.
Rem dirimet Balbus. Balbum furialiter odi.
    Qui color est Balbi, non erit ille meus.

## MIDSUMMER

Nunc calor est ingens; rapido nunc torridus aestu
    sol furit, et nobis membra vigore carent.
Corpus iners sedeo; toto de corpore sudor
    stillat, apud culinas ut fluit assa caro.
Vix oculis utor, vix auribus; omnia sordent,
    ipsaque mens languet victaque ponit onus.
A quoties fluvii succurrit amabile frigus,
    a quoties gelida pocula mixta citro.
Ignosco rabiem furiosaque dicta magistris;
    hos quoque—sunt homines—torquet acuta sitis.

## A FAILURE

Esse velim pictor.  Maior scit pingere frater
    et varias facili res simulare manu.
Invideo spectans.  Calamo describit acuto
    automatos currus aeriasque rates.
Vix tetigit cartam: vivunt animalia passim;
    hic catuli currunt, hic agitantur equi.
Et comitum mira referuntur imagine voltus;
    en, Bruti dentes, oraque sima Titi.
Est quoque cuiusdam facies sub clave magistri.
    O quantos risus ista tabella movet.
De me nil potuit.  Pueri risere, catello
    tam similem fecit dissimilemque mihi.

## DULCE DOMUM

Si volucres hominum redduntur ab aere voces
    et capitur distans quilibet aure sonus,
cur ad doctores patria de sede redimus
    nec dictata licet discere verba domi?
Quot solvi poterunt incommoda. Quanta facultas
    sic datur ut cunctis dulcius adsit opus.
Vnus erit doctor; pueri, tot milia, discent;
    inde, pater, sumptus causa minoris ero.
Erudiar paucis (iam nulla viatica poscam)
    assibus. O ditem me remorante domum.
Rem, precor, inventam volvas, pater optime, tecum;
    hoc in proposito nonnihil esse reor.

## ECLIPSE OF THE SUN

Turbabam populos exstincto lumine quondam,
    venturique dabam tristia signa mali.
Corda hominum steterant; reges et sceptra cadebant;
    arma metu victi deposuere duces.
Nunc nimium docti rerum cognoscere causas
    exspectant homines praecipiuntque diem.
Astrologi signant obliquo limite terras.
    Huc coeunt cives visaque rara petunt.
Et pueris—pueri discunt nunc omnia—fio
    ridiculus, proavis qui timor ante fui.
'Aspice', conclamant, 'veterem, pater, aspice solem.
    Quam bene post lunam condidit ille caput.'

## Κρεῖσσον σιωπᾶν

Qui ratione carent homines sine fine loquuntur;
    qui sapiunt clauso saepius ore tacent.
Aureus Harpocrates deus est, argenteus Hermes;
    plus quam posse loqui posse tacere valet.
Aurea contentis servate silentia linguis;
    sic incorruptas accumulatis opes.
Divitiae mentis crescunt; sapientia floret;
    saepe venit pressa voce reperta salus.
Insidias vulpis quam saepe cuniculus olim
    vitavit quoniam dixerat ipse nihil.
Instituit Natura duas mortalibus aures;
    addidit os unum. Quid velit, inde patet.


## A BAD DAY

Mane torum, credo, laeva de parte reliqui;
    omnia per totum prava fuere diem.
Principio torquem rupi caligaeque ligamen;
    tum secui digitum, forte labante manu.
Postmodo displicui (nec erat mea culpa) magistro;
    nunc redit in dentem perditus ille dolor.
Adde quod amisi bis sex asinaliter asses.
    Diluvies, aiunt, est ubicunque pluit.
Una prius me res, tum me res altera damnat,
    et mala succedunt continuata malis.

## MAGNUM IN PARVO

Non semper magnis accedit gloria rebus;
    saepe est in parvo corpore maior honos.
Scilicet exiguis ornantur floribus agri;
    quaeritur ex imo baca minuta mari.
Ponitur exemplo longi formica laboris;
    et quo sint animo testificantur apes.
Nonne breves pueri vincunt certamine longos?
    nonne gerunt parvi munera magna viri?
Mus olim potuit capto prodesse leoni;
    et periit Iacci victus ab arte gigas.
I nunc, Ambiorix, validos ostende lacertos.
    Et mihi sunt nervi, nec sine mente caput.


## WINTER COMES

Nunc Natura dolet; moritur miserabilis annus;
    flore carent horti; stat sine fronde nemus.
Non ita nos pueri mutata sorte dolemus;
    gaudia nimbosus multa November habet.
Dormiat her hiemem; placeant sua somnia gliri.
    Appetit humanum nobiliora genus.
Nos iuvat in campo pedibus propellere follem;
    et brevior patitur discere plura dies.
Excipimus comites pluvias et flamina caeli;
    et mens exemplo corporis ipsa viget.
Annus obit. Noster stimulatur frigore sanguis.
    Terra dolet. Nobis aspera ridet hiems.

## CHANGING MOODS

Martius ancipiti conturbat numine caelum;
    miscet Hyperboreas sole notoque nives.
Nunc patulos verrit glaciali flamine campos,
    nunc revocat zephyros ambrosiosque dies.
Induit hibernos voltus: stat frigore sanguis;
    induit aestivos: crura manusque tepent.
Sic aliquem vidi placidam componere frontem
    et sibi ridendo conciliare suos.
Continuo sensi nulla ratione furentem
    dictaque iactantem frigidiora gelu.
Tempora se mutant; habitu mutamur eodem,
    et vario subitas sumimus ore vices.

## YES AND NO

Aurea cum calidis arridet solibus aestas,
    et rapidus siccos Sirius urit agros,
tum tepidas homines ripas et litora quaerunt;
    in fluvio ludunt caeruleove mari.
Abiciunt vestes pueri iuvenesque senesque,
    et populus nudo corpore findit aquas.
Progenitus nautis si nescit nare Britannus,
    indecorat gentem scilicet ipse suam.
'Nasne, puer?' dixi: visebam forte nepotem;
    hoc volui primum discere—'Nasne, puer?'
'No' mihi respondit. 'Non no' si verba fuissent,
    aureus in zona nunc remaneret avi.

## VERY PRECIOUS

En, quot sunt homines qui me curare iubentur;
    en, mihi, ne peream, quanta parata cohors.
Nonne coquit pistor panem dulcesque placentas
    et lanius pingues mactat amicus oves?
Me meditans olitor longo serit ordine caules;
    ne nimis esuriam, pisa fabasque colit.
Ne sitiam, tenero pascuntur gramine vaccae
    et super aequoreas navita currit aquas.
Dat caligas sutor, molles dat textor amictus;
    tonsor adest prudens, ne nimis hirtus eam.
Advolat aegroto medicus; dexterrimus alter
    dentibus invigilans praevenit omne malum.
Circum stant famulique simul doctique magistri.
    Quanti sim patriae, quis dubitare potest?

## SMALL BEGINNINGS

Rupe sub ignota qui fons tenuissimus exit,
    volvet inoffensas maximus amnis aquas.
Vertice quae tangit nubes altissima quercus,
    glans prius obscura parva latebat humo.
Innocuus tacito catulus ludebat in antro
    terribili magnus qui rudit ore leo.
Non subito parva crescunt ab origine vires;
    ipsa suis alitur gloria longa moris.
Magnus Alexander, credo, puerilibus annis
    non dispar nobis dissimilisve fuit.
Par mihi Caesar erat, recitans elementa magistro;
    par mihi, dum temptat carmina prima, Maro.

## THE WEATHER

Nunquam non homines de tempestate loquuntur;
    scilicet hic sermo taedia nulla facit.
Post aliquod tempus sordere negotia constat
    cetera: materies ista perire nequit.
Improba Tempestas, toto variabilis anno,
    immerito magnas vincis honore deas.
Plurima te crebris agitant convivia linguis,
    et resonat tota nomen in urbe tuum.
Me tamen irritas; me non intellegis unum;
    aure meas surda spernis iniqua preces.
Discere si cogor, passim sine nube renides;
    ludere cum licuit, nube referta pluis.


## DONE AFTER ALL

Caecilius vester, pueri, residebat in hortis,
    promissum faciens quod faceretis opus.
Sole fruebatur; calvum caput aura fovebat;
    fons aderat; murmur molle sonabat apum.
Pransus erat; vini calicem potaverat unum;
    naribus adnabat floris amicus odor.
Omnia suadebant requiem somnumque poetae;
    sensim oculos clausit deposuitque caput.
Praetereunt pedibus tacitae velocibus horae;
    Caecilio versus surripit ille sopor.

Rem memorat: veniunt numeri, mirabile dictu,
    et factum carmen, quod faciatis, adest.

## STAMPS

Ecce, liber splendet positis ex ordine signis;
    ecce, suum monstrat pagina quaeque decus.
Non paribus decorant reginae floribus hortos;
    non latet in gazis par diadema meo.
Quot varias facies cernis mixtosque colores.
    Nomina nummorum quot peregrina legis.
Praecipue tueor quas raras insula quaedam
    protulit effigies. Vnus et alter habent.
Interea disco gentes et nomina regum,
    et venit ignaro cognitionis amor.
I nunc, disce, Mari, collectas figere blattas.
    I nunc, ova avium sugere disce, Cato.

## THE FAT BOY

Pinguis Anaxagoras nullo non tempore dormit;
    et manet irruptus nocte dieque sopor.
Distribuunt alii varias aequaliter horas;
    ille solet nocti continuare diem.
Si monet Orbilius, monitis non applicat aurem;
    si ludos agimus, vix movet ille pedem.
Nil valet arreptum digitis convellere crinem,
    nil valet inserta pungere corpus acu.
Tum redit ad sensus, et tum vigilare videtur,
    cum vocat ad positas buccina rauca dapes.
Tunc oculos aperit; puero tum membra moventur;
    et comites clamant 'Vivit Anaxagoras'.

## BEAST AND BOY

Ad severum quemdam et iniustum magistrum et
Naturae legum, mea sententia, parum perspicacem.

Quandocunque libet reddunt animalia vocem
    cetera. Me linguam, Prisce, tenere iubes.
Hinnit equus, si vult; si vult, dat murmura felis;
    latrat inexpletus nocte dieque canis.
Quam stimulat Natura, nefas inhibere loquellam.
    Quis vetat, in spurca sus ubi grunnit hara?
Quolibet in prato (nescis?) bos libera mugit;
    quolibet in clivo libera balat ovis.
Altera lex pecudi, puero lex altera constat.
    Num tam diversi dissimilesque sumus?
Cum rudit, aurito nemo indignatur asello.
    Dicere quod volui cur ego, Prisce, vetor?

## THE AVERAGE BOY

Immerito duris quidam mediocria dictis
    ingenia illudunt opprobriisque notant.
Vtilis est miles, si non est optimus armis;
    utilis est, si non optimus arte, faber.
Pauci summa tenent; plures referuntur ad imum;
    in medio restat maxima turba loco.
Magni saepe viri partes egere secundas;
    nec, fateor, tanti me pudet esse gregis.
Praeterea quoties hominum sententia vincit
    qui stant in stratis praetereuntve viis.
Nec puer indoctus, nec sum doctissimus idem.
    'In medio Virtus' dixit Aristoteles.

## THE INDIAN TEAM

Ecce, colorati veniunt distantibus Indi
    finibus. Hesperia certat Eoa manus.
Auriferos montes et eburna palatia linquunt
    et sacras urbes indigenasque deos.
Purpureis illic splendent pavonibus horti,
    et decorant regum gemmea tecta domos.
Terribili densae serpunt ibi tigride silvae;
    turrigero spissae stant elephante viae.
Ipsa suos frustra mirabilis India captat.
    Huc veniunt, nostrae dedita turba pilae.
Huc veniunt lusum; magni cupiuntur honores;
    pax alitur ludis et fit amica fides.


## NOTHING LEFT

### I

Iudice me, comites, nostra est mirabilis aetas.
    Ingenio scimus vincere quidquid obest.
Ecce, mihi lucent icto sine sulfure lychni.
    Ecce, mihi nullo raeda movetur equo.
Aerias hominum longe deprendere voces
    possumus et cantu colloquioque frui.
Conspicuo solidos penetramus lumine muros;
    est nova vis oculis; cernimus acta procul.
Transvolat oceanum tutis nunc Icarus alis;
    tuta sub aequoreis navis oberrat aquis.
Ipse ego quod faciam doleo nihil esse relictum.
    Magnus Alexander cuncta subacta queror.

## NOTHING LEFT

### II

Quid, mea Musa, canam, quod non cecinere poetae?
  Non iam materies carminis ulla manet.
Sive cano virides campos undasque loquaces,
  sive nigros montes caeruleosque lacus,
sive fretum memoro pulsataque litora fluctu,
  sive per immensum sidera mota polum,
sive feras pecudumque genus pictasque volucres
  et quali salsae pisce natantur aquae;
sive placet tostas segetes et munera Pacis,
  sive ferum duri dicere Martis opus;
haec alii cecinere; aliorum versibus uti
  me pudeat. Nolo scribere. Musa, tace.


## IT'S NOT THE COAT—

Parve puer, vesti nimium ne crede decorae;
  non facit ingenuum palla superba virum.
Saepe tegunt viles fortissima pectora panni;
  saepe latet picta mens inhonesta toga.
Non semel aspexi iuvenes prodire per urbem
  vestibus in nitidis et sine mente tamen.
Quid trepido prosunt virgatae tempore bracae?
  quid tibi lucidior papilione chlamys?
Indociles veniant habitus et sponte sequantur,
  ipse suo qualis flore renidet ager.
Tu bonus et simplex esto promptusque labori,
  et tua, ni fallor, par tibi vestis erit.

## THE SIXTH SENSE

Aspicio campos oculis et sidera caeli
    et varias artes pulcraque facta virum.
Auribus excipio mixtas testudine voces
    et comitum risus Orbiliique iocos.
Multa placent tactu; gratus mihi frigidus amnis
    solstitio, bruma gratus ab igne calor.
Delicias haurit nasus fumante culina,
    et tenerae blando gaudet odore rosae.
Multa meo semper veniunt iucunda palato,
    praecipue vester, dulcia fraga, sapor.
Quinque habeo sensus. Addat Sapientia sextum,
    ne sitiam tantas aridus inter opes.

## POETA FIT NON NASCITUR

Me melius Naso, quo non facundior alter,
    carmen in undenos digerit arte pedes.
Vergilium, fateor, non possum vincere cantu.
    Me melius memorat pascua, rura, duces.
Si citharam sumpsi, Flacco cantante relinquor;
    nec par sum numeris, docte Catulle, tuis.
Spe tamen incendor; veterum vestigia servo;
    hos sequor et pono qua posuere gradum.
Sic pueri summas sensim ducuntur ad artes;
    sic facili musa convenienter eunt.
Ipse ego mox hedera viridi mea tempora nectam,
    Pierii vates creditus esse chori.

## RELATIVITY

En, per se nihil est, et ab omnibus omnia pendent;
    multaque mutantur tempore, multa loco.
Ludimus, et rapitur tempus properantibus alis;
    discimus, et tardum vix trahit hora pedem.
Iure nigro gaudent inter ieiunia reges;
    si facerent epulas, respueretur idem.
Si Catulus cantat, vox est dulcissima corvi;
    Clodius est pulcer cum sedet ante Lupum.
Prae pueris dicas sapientes esse magistros;
    et mus prae minimo pulice magnus erit.
Quod cibus est aliis, aliis est acre venenum;
    nec miseri comedunt dulcia pruna senes.
Omnia sunt aliis maiora minoraque rebus;
    re fert quo fiant tempore quoque loco.


## CROSS-WORDS

Vndique nunc homines cruciformia verba resolvunt;
    de solido partem mos capit ille die.
Nec stulti faciunt; doctissima turba virorum
    huic operi passim dedita tota sedet.
Causidici cessant et rupta negotia linquunt;
    utraque deserta est curia; castra silent.
Credere si fas est, mediis sermonibus errant
    pontifices, si vox forte petita subit.
Saepe sedent nostri contracta fronte magistri
    dum tacitos agimus, cauta caterva, iocos.
At, quales, rogitas? cocto properatius ovo
    solvimus occultas nos quoque, Marce, cruces.

## STRIKE AT ONCE

Rem decide, puer, simul est oblata facultas;
    saepe suis veniunt facta pericla moris.
Expedit urticam pressa comprendere dextra;
    intrepidis nullus redditur inde dolor.
Occupat iratum quisquis per cornua taurum,
    praevenit incolumis multa futura mala.
Tunde prius candens—tunc est tractabile—ferrum
    quam redeat durus, qui fuit ante, rigor.
Verbere non tardo praestat truncare colubram;
    sic perit e diris faucibus atra lues.
Pone moras semper; primas exstingue favillas;
    una prius totam stravit omissa domum.


## CORONATION DAY, 1935

Si minimo fas est puero, Rex Quinte Georgi,
    versibus et plausu te celebrare meo,
hoc inquam: Rector non est sapientior usquam,
    non est quem populus tam vehementer amat.
Omnibus in terris turbat violentia leges;
    sceptra cadunt; multo regnat in orbe Timor.
Tu trepidas inter gentes saevosque tumultus
    imperio miti litora mille beas.
a.d. x Quint. nostra Kal.
    tergeminis grates dat schola tota sonis.
'Vivat Rex', canimus—quatitur clamoribus aether—
    'Adiciat lustris altera quinque suis.'
'Vivat Rex', canimus; 'Rex est hilarisque bonusque';
    et fruimur vacuo, libera turba, die.

## EVELYNS

*(School Chronicle)*

Mitis ades, Clio; parvi dum magna movemus,
    mitis ades; res est numine digna tuo.
Hi fac ut annales in postera saecula vivant
    nostraque per terras fama superstes eat.
Illustres erimus, si tu, dea magna, favebis,
    et fiet, quidquid scribimus, historia.
Non ignorabit, qui simus, serior aetas,
    nec tacita noster nocte premetur honor.
Evelynae nomen longos resonabit in annos
    non sine Praepositi nomine Vorselii.

## AVE ATQUE VALE

Nuper, Grosphe, 'Vale, placens Etona'
vix prae fletibus eloquens obortis,
nunc inter lacrimas micante risu,
'Formosissima Magdalena, salve',
tot plaudentibus optimis amicis
multa non sine gratulatione,
dico spe radians novisque rebus.

## BEAUTY AND THE BEAST

### I

Lux electrica, noctis administra,
admirabile sidus in tenebris,
qui fit tam tibi turpis ut parens sit?
Cur tam difficilis venis ab alvo,
cur tam duriter ac laboriose?
Pulcra es, confiteor, sed ista mater
est immanior omnibus chimaeris;
nec te enititur in modum pudicum;
sed turpi gemitu maloque fumo
noctem non leviter diemque turbat,
et fuligine foedat arboreta,
unde et tu, mea Magdalena, sordes,
qua nil dulcius est amoeniusve.

### II

Lux electrica, noctis administra,
sic candore novo per hos recessus,
nigrae filia matris enitescas,
sic te non pudeat tuae parentis
et solvat tibi Magdalena grates,
sic me nocte bees meosque praesens,
absens nascere me procul meisque.

## APOPHORETA

*Thermos*

Sive premit frigus, de me, Torquate, calorem,
    sive calor vexat, frigora grata bibe.

*Pocket-mirror*

Hoc licet in speculo, si vis, formose, decorem
    cernere, nec timor est ullus Hamadryadum.

*Corkscrew*

Ad vinum sitiens presso sub cortice clausum
    non sine me certam scis aperire viam.

*Shaving-soap*

Spuma decet pulcros iuvenes—procul este, Catones;
    diligit hirsutas nulla puella genas.

*Ash stick*

Non opus est gladio. Quoties spatiaris in agro,
    haec soleat tecum fraxinus ire comes.

*Sloe-gin*

Admiscenda mero silvestria pruna leguntur
    ut tu me pransus, dulcis amice, bibas.

*Note-case*

En, gaza in parvo; parvum nec inutile munus
    vult in deliciis esse sinuque tuo.

*Paper-knife*

Quo prius in silvis elephas fera bella gerebat,
    nunc tenues cartas leve secabit ebur.

*Ledger*

Ad nummum constet ratio; refer omnia nobis;
    ni conturbaris, res tibi grandis erit.

*Pack of cards*

En, fustes tibi sunt, adamantes, corda, ligones;
    vincere te iubeat regius ille ligo.

## 28

## A. D. G.

[*Reliquiae.* A. D. GODLEY. EDITED BY C. R. L. FLETCHER]

Lector, si quis est in te literarum cultus,
sive adulescens es sive es adultus,
saepe tecum dixeris 'Hercule, quam multus
hoc in libro sensus est ioculis sepultus'.

Perlegant discipuli, perlegant tutores;
hos et illos faciet multo meliores;
his et illis corriget eleganter mores,
et aprico monitu abiget dolores.

Quod in his sermonibus cunque disputatur,
scriptor iste pius est nec nefanda fatur;
si quid improbandum est, risu improbatur;
doctus et iocosus est; docte ioculatur.

Idem si quid queritur, mitis est querella,
quamvis facto pereat igne multa sella,
de Responsionibus fulminet procella,
artium admissa sit titulo puella.

Aequat iste Socratem lepido sermone;
aequat Aristotelem disputatione;
aemulatur Pindarum numeris; egone
fallor an orator est maior Cicerone?

Ore de re publica disserit facundo;
more de Motore Bo canit laetabundo;
nulla tam hilariter sonuit arundo;
nihil numerosius toto est in mundo.

Hic est sapientia tibi profutura,
dulce mel et merum sal et voluptas pura;
adde quod doctissimi editoris cura
omne desiderium sustulit. Quid plura?

[Width and Wisdom here you'll find (who can do without it?),
Salt and honey, mere delight (who that reads can doubt it?),
Quite a decent editor. Well, sir, what about it? C. R. L. F.]

## O FACTUM MALE

Lugete, atria sancta Magdalenae
et qui discitis aut docetis istic;
nostri psittacus occidit Magistri,
quem plus ille oculis suis amabat,
qui maturius evocare lecto
et cantu dominum sequi solebat
per quantaslibet occupationes
et furtim vetitum crepare nomen
et non dissimiles referre voces.
Nunc est tota domus sepulta luctu
quae laetis modo canticis sonabat;
vox obmutuit illa 'quid moraris?'
vox obmutuit illa 'me venustum',
nec 'felem' resonant, ut ante, 'felem'
aedes quot varios habent recessus.
Nunc est undique vasta solitudo
et fletus hominum gravesque voltus
insolabiliter deos rogantum
'tantas delicias quid abstulistis?
Tanta haec nostra quid occidit voluptas
nunc desiderio dolenda longo?'

## AMICABILIS CONCORDIA

Magdalena, quid in solo
pauper et tenuis iaces?
Surge, supprime lacrimas,
    laetos indue voltus.

Ecce, purpureo via est
picta vere tuum in decus;
dives, aurea prodeas,
    O amata et amanda.

Grandis in viridario
lilia inter et irides
prodeas domina ac tuorum
    audias bona dicta.

Haec et illa tibi domus
iungit hospitio suos;
hinc et inde, beata, te
    prosequuntur alumni.

Vsque laetior in dies
edita ad geminorum aquas
fluminum populo potens
    praesidebis utrique.

Vsque carius in dies
dulce nomen amabimus
Magdalena, tuam in fidem
    dedicata iuventus.

## AD ADULESCENTES

### I

Laetus ago grates quod tam studiosa librorum
    tamque memor Tripodis scribitur ista cohors.
Me si conicitis molli recubare sub umbra,
    fallimini; durum me quoque versat opus.
Mane manus languet scriptis; tum sessile corpus
    exstimulo, nimius si minuatur adeps.
Ingentes scando scopulos; ingentia rura
    pervolito pedibus duplicibusque rotis.
Sera tamen cena est, et amicos quinque saluto,
    et 'cyathos' inquam 'da mihi quinque, puer'.

### II

Vt ille mergus, i volans, epistula,
fideliterque dic meis sodalibus
amica dicta cum salute plurima.
'Bonus magister iste' nunties velim
'valet, renidet, otiosus ambulat,
fideque maius acquiescit ad focum
ioco meroque plenus.' O quid aequius
seni putatur esse? Iunioribus
'Inertiam cavete' dic, epistula,
'cavete pocula et dapes et otium,
iuvetque rebus interesse seriis.
Lychnos replete, perpolite calceos,
cremanda ligna findite, et scientiae
studete semper.' Est enim laboribus
iuventa nata; carpimus senes rosas.

## AD ADULESCENTES

### III

#### THE PUZZLE

*Oedipus Sphinxin salutem*

Vni discipuli novem Magistro
nuper difficilem dolum parantes,
ipso ne miser otio vacaret,
'Hoc aenigmate magnus ille doctor',
dicebant hilari strepente risu,
'perturbabitur et profana dicet
(olim tam bonus et pius Magister)
et scalpet caput et deos vocabit,
et nos nostraque devovebit Orco,
haec cum non poterit sepulta verba
tantis e tenebris resuscitare'—
ignari, neque enim suo sciebant
quantum esset domino latinitatis:
qui nullum capitis movens capillum,
sed molli recubans super cathedra,
inter colloquium et merum iocumque,
structum vix opus undecim diebus
(pulcrum, Iuppiter, et laboriosum)
una continuo resolvit hora,
tanto doctior eruditiorque
unus discipulis novem Magister.


## TO HANDEL

#### PROFESSOR DENT AT HALLE, FEB. 23, 1935

Magne pater cantus, qua te pietate colamus,
quo sit apud Camum vox in honore tua,
hanc ego collectam nostra de fronde coronam
cantoresque mei ponimus indicium.

# 33

## FOR LATIN ELEGIACS

### I

All things hungry Time devours;
  Walls of cities broken lie;
Bricks and mortar fade like flowers;
  Poems never die.

Towers crumble in the dust;
  Temples made of marble fall;
Iron perishes with rust;
  Song outlives them all.

### II

The pleasant hours too quickly run,
When all our world is bright with sun;
But slow they drag, and long they stay,
When clouds have overcast the day.

Yet Time proceeds with pace the same;
That scythed old man is not to blame;
'Tis we extend the shades of night
And put our joys too soon to flight.

### III

Alone went Astor unafraid;
His way was wrapped in dreadful shade;
Inwoven boughs shut out the sun,
And light to mark his path was none;
Yet eyes of lions seemed to glow,
And wolves through all the wood to go;
Phantoms were moving here and there;
Faces he saw with bloody hair.
But Resolution steeled his breast;
With faithful heart right on he pressed.
'These Terrors—if I give them heed,'
Thought he, 'I shall be lost indeed.'

## THE INQUIRER

γῆς ἐφίλεις τόδε χρῆμα τὸ δαίδαλον, οὐδ᾽ ἀπολήγειν
  ἤθελες ἓν πάντων μὴ σὺ διεξετάσας
τούτων ὅσσα πέρ ἐστι κεκρυμμένα· νῦν δὲ μαθήσει
  ἄλλο τι καὶ τούτων μεῖζον ἀποιχόμενος.


This intricate earth you loved.  You would not rest
Till all its hidden points should stand your test.
And now your spirit, parted from it, sees
Another world and greater things than these.

I strove with none, for none was worth my strife;
  Nature I loved, and, next to Nature, Art;
I warmed both hands before the fire of life;
  It sinks, and I am ready to depart.

LANDOR.


οὐκ ἐς ἔριν πέπτωκα· τί γὰρ πλέον; ἄξιος οὐδείς·
  ἤρασμαι φύσεως καὶ μετὰ τήνδε τέχνης·
ἄμφω χεῖρας ἔθαλπον ἐπ' ἐσχαρεῶνι βίοιο,
  ψυχομένου δ' ὑπάγω τοῦ πυρὸς οὐκ ἀέκων.

When first my ways to fair I took
    Few pence in purse had I,
And long I used to stand and look
    At things I could not buy.

Now times are altered: if I care
    To buy a thing, I can;
The pence are here and here's the fair,
    But where's the lost young man?

To think that two and two are four,
    And neither five nor three,
The heart of man has long been sore
    And long 'tis like to be.

A. E. HOUSMAN.

Bis bina quot sint, Hortale, non semel
experta ab usu mens hominum, et pari
   quid desit impar, quid supersit,
      iam nimis indoluit, nimisque,

credo, indolescet saucia.  Me prius
festis petentem temporibus forum,
   me stantem et haerentem tuendo
      scruta tribus meliora nummis

mutavit aetas.  Nunc bene compoti
quidvis parantis, si placuit, rei
   est aeris, est festi facultas;
      ille fuit iuvenilis emptor.

Thus the craftsman thinks to grace the rose—
      Plucks a mould-flower
      For his gold flower,
Uses fine things that efface the rose.

Rosy rubies make its cup more rose,
      Precious metals
      Ape the petals—
Last some old king locks it up morose!

Then how grace a rose? I know a way!
      Leave it rather.
      Must you gather?
Smell, kiss, wear it—at last throw away.

R. BROWNING.

Quo rosam pacto decores, Lycori,
quaeris? Exstinxit faber exprimendo
scilicet sumpta pretiosiorem,
    fingere iactans

auream, gazis quod acerbus aevo
conderet Mygdon simulante frondes
bractea splendens opus et rubentis
    orbe pyropi.

Crede consulto. Potior venustas
vivet intactae. Legis? ore libans
naribus subdas, decores gerendo,
    proiciasque.

If all the good people were clever,
  And all clever people were good,
The world would be nicer than ever
  We thought that it possibly could.

But somehow, 'tis seldom or never
  The two hit it off as they should;
The good are so harsh to the clever,
  The clever so rude to the good.

E. WORDSWORTH.

Ingenium semper si cum pietate vigeret
   nullaque non pietas ingeniosa foret,
viveret hoc quodcunque hominum est iucundius, Hirti,
   posse prius fieri quam fuit ulla fides.
Nunc fit ut aut raro pariter (quod oportet) eodem
   aut nunquam coeant subter utrique iugo.
Tu premis ingenium, pietas, nimis aspera iudex;
   tu nimis insultas, ingeniose, piis.

God makes sech nights, all white an' still
    Fur'z you can look or listen,
Moonshine an' snow on field an' hill,
    All silence an' all glisten.

Zekle crep' up quite unbeknown,
    An' peeked in thru' the winder,
An' there sot Huldy all alone,
    'ith no one nigh to hender.

The very room, coz she was in,
    Seemed warm from floor to ceilin',
An' she looked full ez rosy agin
    Ez the apples she was peelin'.

He was six foot o' man, A 1,
    Clear grit an' human natur';
None couldn't quicker pitch a ton
    Nor dror a furrer straighter.

He'd sparked it with full twenty gals,
    He'd squired 'em, danced 'em, druv 'em,
Fust this one, an' then thet, by spells—
    All is, he couldn't love 'em.

But long o' her his veins 'ould run
    All crinkly like curled maple,
The side she breshed felt full o' sun
    Ez a south slope in Ap'il.

LOWELL.

Est ubi, quantum oculos, quantum contenderis aures,
    nox micat, et iussit cuncta silere deus.
Sic nive tum stabant lunae sub lumine campi,
    sic iuga, dum tacitis lux manet una locis.
Pyramus adrepsit furtim, rimamque petenti
    praebuit angustam parva fenestra viam.
Ante oculos Thisbe nullo comitante sedebat;
    colloquium nemo qui prohiberet erat.
At domus interior, tam dulcis conscia formae,
    tota novis visa est intepuisse modis.
Poma secat cultro: pomis magis ipsa rubescit;
    his color est roseus: pulcrior illa rosis.
Grandior ante alios iuvenis, sine crimine corpus,
    integra cui virtus simplicitasque vigent.
Scit nemo citius plaustris imponere messem;
    vomere tam recto non secat alter humum.
Blanditiis multas captaverat ante puellas—
    testantur facilem raeda chorusque procum—
sed desultor erat; nunc haec, nunc illa placebat;
    omnia si fecit, defuit unus amor.
Huic simul adsedit, trepidabant sanguine venae,
    haud secus ac venas tortile crispat acer;
ac velut austrinus tepido mons ridet Aprili,
    Thisbe quam tetigit, pars ea sole calet.

O! the spring-time of life is the season of blooming,
   And the morning of love is the season of joy,
Ere noontide and summer, with radiance consuming,
   Look down on their beauty, to parch and destroy.

O! faint are the blossoms life's pathway adorning,
   When the first magic glory of hope is withdrawn;
For the flowers of the spring, and the light of the morning,
   Have no summer budding, and no second dawn.

Through meadows all sunshine, and verdure, and flowers,
   The stream of the valley in purity flies;
But mix'd with the tides, where some proud city lowers,
   O! where is the sweetness that dwelt on its rise?

The rose withers fast on the breast it first graces;
   Its beauty is fled ere the day be half done:
And life is that stream which its progress defaces
   And love is that flower which can bloom but for one.

PEACOCK.

Vere suo florent homines viridique iuventa;
    et sua mane suo gaudia sentit amor.
Mox Canis et medio vexat sol aethere flagrans,
    et decus aspectu torridiore necat.
Inde hominum languent circum vestigia flores
    sidereum pressit spes ubi prima iubar;
nam neque verna tument aestivo germina fetu,
    altera nec sero lux venit orta die.
Pascua flore nitent, et aprico gramine valles,
    qua rapitur pura lympha corusca via;
mox ea lympha caret primi dulcedine fontis
    urbs ubi corruptis imminet alta fretis.
Cui rosa primus honos, in eodem pectore marcet;
    ante iacet medio quam stetit axe dies.
Quae rosa tam brevis est? qui sic perit amnis eundo?
    amnis vita hominum est; flos, breve nomen, Amor.

Some the degraded slaves of lust,
Prostrate and trampled in the dust,
   Shall rise no more;
Others, by guilt and crime, maintain
The scutcheon that without a stain
   Their fathers bore.

Wealth and the high estate of pride,
With what untimely speed they glide,
   How soon depart!
Bid not the shadowy phantoms stay,
The vassals of a mistress they,
   Of fickle heart.

These gifts in Fortune's hands are found;
Her swift revolving wheel turns round,
   And they are gone!
No rest the inconstant goddess knows,
But changing, and without repose,
   Still hurries on.

Even could the hand of avarice save
Its gilded baubles, till the grave
   Reclaimed its prey,
Let none on such poor hopes rely;
Life, like an empty dream, flits by,
   And where are they?

The pleasures and delights, which mask
In treacherous smiles life's serious task,
   What are they, all,
But the fleet coursers of the chase,
And death an ambush in the race,
   Wherein we fall?

LONGFELLOW.

Hic posuit, domina calcante Libidine, collum;
    turpe iugum patitur, nec levat inde caput;
ille nefanda vetus portans per crimina nomen
    indecorat pulcrae nobilitatis avos.
Dilabuntur opes, altoque superbia voltu
    corruit, et raptim delet acerba dies.
Vana vides; caveas tecum ne ficta morentur
    somnia, periurae turba fidelis erae.
Munifica Fortuna manu sua praemia monstrat;
    dispereunt verso cum volat orbe rota.
Non eadem est unquam, sed vi dea semper eadem
    urget iter, demptis praecipitata moris.
Et si delicias et inane tueberis aurum
    dum pereas, Orco rem repetente suam—
proposito sit nulla fides; quasi noctis imago
    vita fugit; quae tum spes erat, ista fuit.
Blanda voluptatum facies; mendacia rident;
    eripe personam: seria vita subest.
His certatur equis; rapimur, factaque ruina
    excidimus positas Mortis in insidias.

There are whose study is of smells,
  Who to attentive schools rehearse
What something mixed with something else
  Makes something worse.

Some cultivate in broths impure
  The clients of our body; these,
Increasing without Venus, cure
  Or cause disease.

Others the heated wheel extol,
  And all its offspring, whose concern
Is how to make it farthest roll
  And fastest turn.

Me, much incurious if the hour
  Present, or to be paid for, brings
Me to Brundisium by the power
  Of wheels or wings,

Me, in whose breast no flame hath burned
  Life long, save that by Pindar lit,
Such lore leaves cold; nor have I turned
  Aside for it,

More than when, sunk in thought profound
  Of what the unaltered Gods require,
My steward (friend but slave) brings round
  Logs for my fire.

R. KIPLING.

Natura rerum quae sit odoribus,
intenta sunt quos porticus audiat
   monstrare, vel mixtis duabus
     tertia qua ratione peior
confletur auris. Hic potius rotas
ignemque laudans, unde sit impetus
   maior laborabit volutis
     turbinibus rapidoque rhombo.
Pars efficaces gignere vel luem
sanare nostri corporis incolas
   propagat impurisque nullam
     per venerem generat venenis.
Incurioso non mediocriter,
et nunc et horis damna trahentibus
   alaene me vectent an axes
     Brundisium, mihi, cui quietum
fervore pectus non nisi Pindari,
Naso, per omnes incaluit dies,
   haec prorsus exaudita frigent,
     nec magis alliciunt eodem,
scrutante quam si mente profundius
certo futuri quid placeat deo,
   fert ligna supplendo focorum
     iunctus amicitia minister.

The overfaithful sword returns the user
His heart's desire at price of his heart's blood.
The clamour of the arrogant accuser
Wastes that one hour we needed to make good.
This was foretold of old at our outgoing;
This we accepted who have squandered, knowing,
The strength and glory of our reputations,
At the day's need, as it were dross, to guard
The tender and new-dedicate foundations
Against the sea we fear—not man's award.

> They that dig foundations deep,
>     Fit for realms to rise upon,
> Little honour do they reap
>     Of their generation,
> Any more than mountains gain
> Stature till we reach the plain.
>
> With no veil before their face
>     Such as shroud or sceptre lend—
> Daily in the market-place,
>     Of one height to foe and friend—
> They must cheapen self to find
> Ends uncheapened for mankind.

(continued)

Solvisse votum saepe suo stetit
fidum per ensem sanguine militi;
   verbosus accusator instans
      saepe brevem vitiavit horam
summae potentem. Qui foret exitus
denuntiantem senserat augurem
   Romanus, effuditque prudens
      gentis opes validumque nomen,
duroque largus tempore iudices
sprevit molestos, si nova limina
   tutetur et molles arenas
      fluctibus oppositas tremendis.
Alti minantur suspicientibus
montes ab arvo; non aliter viros
   aeterna fundamenta rerum
      ponere et imperium sagaces
fulcire tuta sede parum sua
laudavit aetas. Scilicet in foro
   et luce, non illi tenentes
      sceptra manu tacitaeque freti
terrore vestis, se pariter gerunt
aequis iniquis, non timidi sua
   pro gente communes per usus
      eximiam reperire causam.

*(continued)*

Through the night when hirelings rest,
　　Sleepless they arise, alone,
The unsleeping arch to test
　　And the o'er-trusted corner-stone,
'Gainst the need, they know, that lies
Hid behind the centuries.

Not by lust of praise or show,
　　Not by Peace herself betrayed—
Peace herself must they forego
　　Till that peace be fitly made;
And in single strength uphold
Wearier hands and hearts acold.

On the stage their act hath framed
　　For thy sports, O Liberty!
Doubted are they and defamed
　　By the tongues their act set free,
While they quicken, tend, and raise
Power that must their power displace.

Lesser men feign greater goals,
　　Failing whereof they may sit
Scholarly to judge the souls
　　That go down into the pit,
And, despite its certain clay,
Heave a new world towards the day.

These at labour make no sign,
　　More than planets, tides or years
Which discover God's design,
　　Not our hopes and not our fears;
Nor in aught they gain or lose
Seek a triumph or excuse.

For, so the Ark be borne to Zion, who
Heeds how they perished or were paid that bore it?
For, so the Shrine abide, what shame—what pride—
If we, the priests, were bound or crowned before it?

R. KIPLING.

Empti quiescit nocte labor gregis;
illi probantes an nimis angulo
    credatur, insomnisve fornix
        quid ferat, advigilant futuris
custodientes abdita saeculis,
nec gloriosa laude nec otio
    capti, sed in veram salutem
        frigida corda manusque lassas
firmare prompti vi propria, sibi
pacem negantes. Qui tua pulpita
    struxere, Libertas, eosdem
        dedecorat populus reosque
explodit, et iam libera civitas
acclamat ipsis qui sibi procreant
    rerum potituros suarum
        seque premunt alios colendo.
Qui magna parvi finximus, arbitri
docti sedentes si quis ad inferos
    decessit, emolimur alte
        tecta novo peritura limo;
illi, quod aestus continuant opus
annive furtim motave sidera,
    mentem laborantes deorum
        non hominum subitas recludunt
spes et timores, nec titulos sibi
rebus secundis nec veniam malis
    poscunt sacerdotes parati
        ferre necem pariter decusque,
non aestimato, dummodo pontifex
scandat triumphans in Capitolium,
    vincti coronatine certam
        sacra vehant initura sedem.

Why gird at Lollius if he care
   To purchase in the city's sight,
With nard and roses for his hair,
   The name of Knight?

Son of unmitigated sires
   Enriched by trade in Afric corn,
His wealth allows, his wife requires,
   Him to be born.

Him slaves shall serve with zeal renewed
   At lesser wage for longer whiles,
And school- and station-masters rude
   Receive with smiles.

His bowels shall be sought in charge
   By learned doctors; all his sons
And nubile daughters shall enlarge
   Their horizons.

For fierce she-Britons, apt to smite
   Their upward-climbing sisters down,
Shall smoothe their plumes and oft invite
   The brood to town.

*(continued)*

Xanthiam, Publi, quod equestre nomen
cum rosis emptum liquidaque nardo
gestiat portare inhiante volgo,
　　　rodere parcas.
Gentis in lucem suboles pudendae
postulat census veniat metendo
Africam vastum cumulantis aurum,
　　　postulat uxor.
Acer in serum famulus diei
serviet parvo; dominum magister
ambiet ludi facilique durus
　　　navita voltu.
Docta curandum iecur Aesculapi
turba captabit; nec adulta proles
nunc in angusto cohibebit amplos
　　　orbe volatus,
aequa iam tactu simul atque plumis
Fulvia ad nidum positis vocabit,
promptior praedae cupidas sorores
　　　sternere rostro.

(*continued*)

For these delights will he disgorge
   The State enormous benefice,
But—by the head of either George—
   He pays not twice!

Whom neither lust for public pelf
   Nor itch to make orations vex—
Content to honour his own self
   With his own cheques—

That man is clean. At least, his house
   Springs cleanly from untainted gold—
Not from a conscience or a spouse
   Sold and resold.

Time was, you say, before men knew
   Such arts, and rose by Virtue guided?
The tables rock with laughter—you
   Not least derided.

R. KIPLING.

Merce pro tali semel iste plenas
hauriens arcas caput atque nomen
Caesaris posthac nihil additurus
      iurat acervo.
Si nec incendit sitis atra fisci
cor nec orandi populum libido,
quisquis est uni sibi non inempti
      largus honoris,
integer vixit: nec enim pudore
fulta venali domus est nec usu
coniugis, puro sed odoris expers
      crevit ab auro.
At gradu cives humiles ab imo
artis ignaros tulit ante virtus
ipsa. Solvuntur tabulae, movente
      te quoque risum.

## TO THE COMPANIONS

Like as the Oak whose Roots descend,
  Through Earth and Stillness, seeking Food
Most apt to furnish in the End
  That dense indomitable Wood

Which, felled, may arm a seaward Flank
  Of Ostia's Mole or—bent to frame
The beaked Liburnian's triple Bank—
  Carry afar the Roman Name:

But which, a Tree, the Season moves,
  Through gentler Gods than Wind or Tide,
Delightedly to harbour Doves,
  Or take some clasping Vine for Bride:

So this Man—prescient to ensure
  (Since, even now, his Orders hold)
A little State should ride secure,
  At Sea, from Foes her Sloth made bold—

Turned in his midmost, harried Round,
  As Venus drove or Liber led,
And snatched from any Shrine he found
  The stolen Draught, the secret Bread.

(continued)

Qualem profundis stirpibus aesculum
telluris alto ducta silentio
   nutrimina obdurant, datura
      roboris indomiti rigorem
unde Ostia ingentem obstruat aggerem
Tyrrheno, et oras nomen in ultimas
   rostrata Romanum Liburna
      tergeminis vehat acta remis—
maritam eandem vitibus et dare
laetam columbis hospitium, deo
   urgente crescentem per annum
      flaminibus meliore et undis:
Plancus ferocem e desidia Patrum
dum sentit hostem et firmat in aequore
   pro gente non magna salutem et
      tempore vix peritura nostro
mandat, tot inter saepe negotia
parens Amori seu duce Libero
   quocunque clam panes repostos
      ex adyto rapuit merumque:

*(continued)*

Nor these alone. His Life betrayed
   No Gust unslaked, no Pleasure missed.
He called the obedient Nine to aid
   The varied Chase. And Clio kissed,

Bidding him write each sordid Love,
   Shame, Panic, Stratagem and Lie,
In full—that Sinners undiscov-
   ered (like Ourselves) might say: ''Tis I!'

R. KIPLING.

his plura furans—nam faciles deas
praedas in omnes evocat, et palam
   iam nulla inexpleta est voluptas,
      nulla fames; et amica Clio
'Sordes pudendas et Venerem et dolos
describe fraudesque' imperat 'et metus,
   ut Flaccus indeprensa peccans
      dicat *ego haec* comitesque Flacci.'

## THE SURVIVAL

Securely, after days
  Unnumbered, I behold
Kings mourn that promised praise
  Their cheating bards foretold.

Of earth-constricting wars,
  Of Princes passed in chains,
Of deeds out-shining stars,
  No word or voice remains.

Yet furthest times receive
  And to fresh praise restore,
Mere breath of flutes at eve,
  Mere seaweed on the shore.

A smoke of sacrifice;
  A chosen myrtle-wreath;
An harlot's altered eyes;
  A rage 'gainst love or death;

Glazed snow beneath the moon;
  The surge of storm-bowed trees—
The Caesars perished soon,
  And Rome Herself: But these

Endure while empires fall
  And Gods for Gods make room....
Which greater God than all
  Imposed the amazing doom?

R. KIPLING.

Iam mihi praeteriens series immensa dierum
        indicat incolumi
saepe duces infecta queri mendacia vatum
        propositumque decus;

ire catenatos reges quid profuit? aut quid
        marte gravi populos
stringi, vel nitidis praeverti sidera factis?
        omnia surda silent;

at vespertino quod spirat flamine lotos,
        at quibus ora natat
algis, excipiunt longissima saecla novisque
        laudibus ingeminant.

Nunc quoque mors animis indignas excitat iras,
        nunc quoque laesus amor;
lecta placet myrtus; fumant altaria donis;
        mutat amica oculos;

luna nives aequat vitreas; aquilone laborans
        aestuat omne nemus;
intereunt maiora: iacet cum Caesare Caesar,
        ipsaque Roma perit:

haec, ubi ponuntur fasces et sceptra, supersunt;
        haec, ubi dis alii
di cedunt aliis, cuius vixere tremendo
        numinis arbitrio?

## THE PORTENT

Oh, late withdrawn from human-kind
   And following dreams we never knew!
Varus, what dream has Fate assigned
   To trouble you?

Such virtue as commends the law
   Of Virtue to the vulgar horde
Suffices not. You needs must draw
   A righteous sword;

And, flagrant in well-doing, smite
   The priests of Bacchus at their fane,
Lest any worshipper invite
   The God again.

Whence public strife and naked crime
   And—deadlier than the cup you shun—
A people schooled to mock, in time,
   All law—not one.

Cease, then, to fashion State-made sin,
   Nor give thy children cause to doubt
That Virtue springs from iron within—
   Not lead without.

R. KIPLING.

Vare, non nostris modo dedicate
somniis, dum sic hominum catervis
exulas, quae te Lachesi probante
    vexat imago?
Iura quae ponit placitura volgo,
ceteris vitae satis apta virtus
sufficit. Tu rem geris ense, recti
    conscius ultor.
Tu nimis dura pietate flagrans,
uvidus ne quo deus advocante
sit redux, ipsam famulos Lyaei
    caedis ad aram.
Inde civilis furor, inde aperta
crimina et, peius cyathis habendum,
omne fas pubes docilis nec unam
    temnere legem.
Lege si fingis scelus, orta ferro
nescio an fallat merito nepotes
extero virtus potuisse plumbo
    credita gigni.

Zidonian Hanno, wandering. . . .
From a slope
That ran bloom-bright into the Atlantic blue . . .
zoned below with cedar-shade,
Came voices like the voices in a dream.

*　　*　　*　　*　　*　　*　　*

Father Hesper, Father Hesper, Watch, watch, ever and aye,
Looking under thy silver hair with a silver eye.
Father, twinkle not thy stedfast sight:
Kingdoms lapse, and climates change, and races die;
Honour comes with mystery;
Hoarded wisdom brings delight.
Number, tell them over, and number
How many the mystic fruit-tree holds,
Lest the red-comb'd dragon slumber
Roll'd together in purple folds.
Look to him, father, lest he wink, and the golden apple be
stol'n away,

(*continued*)

Super alta vectus Hanno celeri rate maria
patria procul relicta vada caerula tetigit
ubi litus omne cingunt cuparissina nemora
et amicta flore multo sola lambit aqua levis.
Ibi molliora somno bibit aure carmina
resonis stupens dearum numeris Hesperidum.
'Pater Hespere,' insonabant, 'Pater Hespere genitor,
Pater Hespere, eia, nobis sine fine vigil ades.
Prospiciat, at cave ne tremebunda sit acies,
ex albidis capillis argenteus oculus.
Pereunt timenda certa vice regna, vice poli,
pereunt sua minutis vice gentibus homines,
sed sacra, cum tacentur, reverentia sequitur,
sapientiaeque magnum volup est reconditae.
Age, tempus, eia, fetus numerare, pater, age,
numerare poma diva quot in arbore niteant.
Cave dormiat, precamur, coluber rutilicomus
furvos in implicato glomerans latere sinus.
Agedum, excita hunc, pater, ne sŏpor occupat oculum,
et mala subtrahat fur auro rubentia;

(continued)

For his ancient heart is drunk with overwatchings night
    and day
Round about the hallow'd fruit-tree curl'd—
Sing away, sing aloud evermore in the wind without stop,
Lest his sealëd eyelid drop,
For he is older than the world.
If *he* waken, *we* waken,
Rapidly levelling eager eyes.
If *he* sleep, *we* sleep,
Dropping the eyelid over our eyes.
If the golden apple be taken
The world will be overwise.
Five links, a golden chain are we,
Hesper, the Dragon, and Sisters three,
Bound about the golden tree.

TENNYSON.

stupet ille enim veterno nimiisque vigiliis
dominatus ut per orbem veterem ipse veterior
cohibet volumine amplo fruticeta sacra sacer.
Recinamus, o sorores; sine fine vaga procul
ferat aura sempiternos cito sibila numeros.
Rapida huic cavete ne nox grave lumen operiat.
Vigilante eo valemus vigilare similiter
aciem citam regentes radiantibus oculis;
simul os reponet aegrum, simul otia aget iners,
subito inde nostra flectet curvus capita sopor.
Agite ergo, ne protervi sapiant nimium homines,
summa simul beatum tueamur ope nemus,
pariter coruscus anguis, pariter erus Hesperus,
pariter trium sororum sociata copula.'

## THE DEAD PARROT

### I

αἴλινον αἴλινον εἰπέ, τεὸν θάλος ἥρπασεν Ἀιδης,
πᾶν δὲ κατήφησεν δῶμ' ὀλοφυρόμενον·
οὐκέτ' ΙΟΥ, ΠΑΙ, ΘΑΣΣΟΝ ἀκούσεαι, οὐκέτι ΡΑΜ ΡΑΜ,
τὴν δὲ πολύφθογγον τύμβος ἄναυδον ἔχει.

C. M. W.

Cry loud. Your house is dazed with grief and gloom,
    For Death has seized your pet. Cry loud and sore.
Your Polly's voice is silent in the tomb;
    'Ram, Ram' and 'Hurry up' you'll hear no more.

### II

μὴ πένθει, φίλε Κριέ, τεὸν θάλος οὐκ ἀπόλωλα,
    ζῶ δ' ἔτ' ἐνὶ σκιεροῖς ἄλσεσι Περσεφόνης,
κἄτι καλῶ ΠΑΙ ΠΑΙ καὶ ΙΟΥ καὶ ΘΑΣΣΟΝ 'ΕΠΕΙΓΟΥ
    καὶ τό γε ΡΑΜ ΡΑΜ ΔΑΜ καὶ τὸ ΔΙΔΩΜΙ ΔΙΔΩΣ.

C. M. W.

    Weep not; for in shade of Elysian glade,
        Dear Ram, yet alive am I.
    I call to the boys with the guttural noise;
        'Hurry up, Hurry up' I cry.
    I am adding a 'Damn' to the old 'Ram, Ram',
        And am learning the verbs in -μι.

## LOS BORRACHOS

Hush! For the youthful arbiter of wine,
  Guilty, with swift suspicion opens wide
  His dark mysterious eyes, and turns aside
To see who dares profane his court divine.

The draught hangs ready for the flagon's brink;
  The jolly shepherd pauses ere he sips,
  With shameless laughter gleaming through his lips.
Come softly hence; come softly; let him drink.


εὐφήμει· θεὸς οἶδεν ὁ κούριος οὑπὶ ποτοῖο,
  οἶδεν ἁλούς, κραιπνῶς δ' ὄμμαθ' ὕποπτα κυκλοῖ
θεσπέσια σκοτόεντα· καὶ ἠνίδε λοξὸς ἐρευνᾷ,
  τίς ποθ' ὁ τολμήσας ἱρὰ βέβηλος ἀθρεῖν.
οἶνος, ἰδού, κρέμαται ποθέων δέπας ἄκρον ἱκέσθαι,
  πρὶν δὲ πιεῖν ποιμὴν ἔσχεθ' ὁ γηθόσυνος,
ἀστράπτει δὲ γέλως φαιδρὸν περὶ χεῖλος ἀναιδής·
  μὴ σύ γε κινήσῃς, ὦ ξένε· σῖγ' ἄπιθι.

                                        C. M. W.

## CHRISTMAS

Quelle est cette odeur agréable,
   Bergers, qui ravit tous nos sens?
S'exhale-t-il rien de semblable
   Au milieu des fleurs du printemps.

Mais quelle éclatante lumière
   Dans la nuit vient frapper nos yeux?
L'astre du jour dans sa carrière
   Fut-il jamais si radieux?

A Bethlehem dans une crêche
   Il vient de vous naître un Sauveur.
Allons! que rien ne vous empêche
   D'adorer votre Rédempteur!

*French Carol.*

Whence is that goodly fragrance flowing,
    Stealing our senses all away?
Never the like did come a-blowing,
    Shepherds, from flow'ry fields in May.

What is that light so brilliant, breaking
    Here in the night across our eyes?
Never so bright the day-star waking
    Started to climb the morning skies!

Bethlehem!—there in manger lying
    Find your Redeemer—haste away!
Run ye with eager footsteps hieing!
    Worship the Saviour born to-day!

## CRESCAM LAUDE RECENS

ODES OF HORACE TRANSLATED BY H. V. M.

Interpres olim me feret ultimos
circum Britannos, Ausonio catus
   a fonte derivare cantus
     Oceano tenus et recenti

lingua.  Renascar clarus ab extero
sermone; voces Anglia redditas
   dictabit, et discent Horati
     carmina cum pueris puellae.


One day a great interpreter shall teach
My verses by another road to reach
   The distant Briton on the ocean shore,
Making them flow in unfamiliar speech.

I shall be born again, and, bright and young,
Shall live translated to another tongue,
   And girls and boys with new delight shall learn
The many tunes by Roman Horace sung.

## THE ROYAL HOTEL

### I

You that light that foul cigar
Where the diners dining are,
Have you not a thought for them?
Have you not a thought at least
For my delicate Yquem
Soiled and sullied from afar
By the breathing of the beast,
Fat and greasy son of Shem
Rising sated from the feast?

### II

Painted lady seated near me,
Though I speak, you cannot hear me.
If you heard me, you would know
(Scarcely gratified, I fear me)
How amazedly I wonder
What it is you will not show;
How perplexedly I ask
What you can have hidden under,
What the face is like below,
More unsightly than the mask.

## THE ROYAL HOTEL

### III

Give me a name wherewith to dub
This quite insufferable cub
With pallid cheek and plastered hair
Who, unadmonish'd and unwhipp'd,
Still in his middle teenage, yet
Poises the gilded cigarette
Or glass intelligently sipp'd,
This sprig ripe for Beelzebub
Who apes the adult, unaware
That somewhere at a bound he skipp'd
The paradise of life, the span
That lies between the child and man,
Nor saw the glory that was there—
And see it now he never can.

## THE PROPHET

Some few that see are eloquent,
And, seated high, command assent;
And some remain below the stairs
Because the vision is not theirs.

And others see the sliding land
Helpless, and tied in tongue and hand,
And may not stir to stay the fall,
And call in vain or not at all.

To sit and watch the error made,
To hold the truth and not persuade,
This is, for man, to learn at length
His weakness, and therein his strength.

## TEESDALE

Now God be praised by me for this,
  That thing so fair I see;
For sight so good, for eyes' delight,
  Now God be praised by me.

For sound of living music, where
  These waters run and fall,
For hearing by the charmëd ear,
  I praise the Lord of all.

I worship him who, making, gave
  The sign, or spoke the word;
Unseen had all this marvel been
  Without him, and unheard.

Name him or not, or what you will;
  Whilst I can hear and see,
Whose hand so e'er this beauty planned,
  That hand is God's for me.

I care not if I know no more;
  Something I hold at least;
And well the windows of my cell
  Lift me above the beast.

If on a rock in lonely space
  Man and his sons are thrown,
Yet sense can catch the symbol whence
  The maker's mind is known.

I will not then escape to doubt,
  Nor hide behind the wall,
Nor moan that nothing can be known
  Because I know not all.

## SIBI CONSTANS

You always say 'I always say—'
At any hour on any day,
By every gust of doctrine blown,
Consistent yet in this alone.

So might a spinning weather-cock
Keep crowing 'I am like a rock'
And, boxing all the compass, cry
'Nought so immoveable as I.'

And men shall say, when you are dead,
'There's nothing that he always said
Except that, any hour or day,
He always said "I always say—".'


## REMORSE

Begone, thou dark Tormentor!
    I will not speak thee fair;
I know thee, old inventor
    Of buried bones of care.

A man, by over-rueing
    Until the set of sun,
May be his own undoing
    With tears for things undone.

## SON, REMEMBER

My son, when thou art not as now,
　But known a prince of men,
Thy riches here and thy good cheer,
　My son, remember then.

Thousands have died unsatisfied
　Who hungered for thy fare;
The thirsty cried, and were denied
　The vintage rich and rare.

'Tis Dives' hell on earth to dwell
　And suffer torment hot,
In long dismay the price to pay
　Of benefits forgot.

And some, alone with tears, have known
　That he who told us true
Of tooth unkind as winter's wind,
　Spake trulier than he knew.

But thou shalt go through fire and foe,
　With memory bright and clean,
Nor greed nor pride from thee shall hide
　The blessings that have been.

And then, my son, when fame is won,
　Thy soul shall heed a voice
That bids thee in the storm and din
　Remember and rejoice.

## DAYLIGHT

Man may dream
Of worn hill and starved stream
If he will.

It comes not soon,
The end begun of darkening moon
And dying sun.

Long night
Comes, and has been. Now is the sight
Of day between.

Not ours to tread
An earth so old, dried, and dead
With endless cold.

And therefore I
Thank this spot of warm sky
God-begot.

This one place
Is ours, this clime pricked in space
And huge time.

Wondering why,
Nor knowing how, we move and die
Here and now.

## THE REMEDY

If the majority
  Always would
Give the priority
  Where it should:

If the inferior
  Public knew
How superior
  Are the few:

If with a humorous
  Will they tossed,
And the more numerous
  Always lost:

England would be
  Out of the wood,
Happy and free,
  Wealthy and good.

Therefore you cleverest
  Brains in the shop,
Conquer this Everest,
  Get to the top.

Now you young sciences,
  Step on the scene,
Fetch your appliances,
  Frame a machine.

Prove that the greater is
  (You who profess
New Numeratories)
  Less than the less.

Here the solution is,
  You who will solve;
Here, Revolution, is
  Stuff to revolve.

## TO A PACIFIST

Claim not alone to tread the track,
　Alone to answer to the call,
Nor bear upon your martyred back
　The universal hope of all.

For they that dare not pay the price,
　Yet preach the gospel for their own,
Do thus blaspheme the sacrifice
　Than which no greater love is known.

## THE SUFFERER

If this you looked to see
　When back the tide was rolled,
Rich victims held in fee,
　An age of gold;

If this was then your goal—
　It lay not in the view
Of some that paid the toll,
　And not a few.

## EMERITUS

I am nearly dead;
  My days darken;
  Few now hearken
To what I said.

Now to recant,
  To turn the coat,
  To burn the boat,
To swell the rant.

Without a doubt
  To flash in the pan
  Is finer than
To fizzle out.

Now for the plat-
  form and the lime-
  light of my prime.
Now I can rat.

Why should I fear
  What may be said?
  Soon I am dead
And cannot hear.

Kept in clover
  By old friends,
  When life ends
I throw them over.

A man, I hold,
  May change his mind,
  However blind,
However old.

## DESIDERATA

You say there was more than appeared
  In his landscape of angles and hooks.
I agree; and I shouldn't have jeered.
  It was lovely except for its looks.

I needn't have had such a fit
  When he sang me his dolorous song.
No doubt it had depth; I admit
  It was only the sound that was wrong.

I never refused to suppose
  That his poem might well have been worse.
I didn't object to its prose,
  But lamented the absence of verse.

## THE GOOD LOSER

In argument or game
  Gravely he takes the blow;
It crosses not his mind to blame
  His fortune or his foe.

His is the certain sun;
  No cramp is here or frost;
Little it matters who has won
  When thus the fight is lost.

## THE WINNER

I love to be the righteous man
    Exalted from the rest,
Provided that the righteous plan
    Will go, with others, west.

The victor victim, sacrificed
    Yet heeding not the cost,
I gladly preach the love of Christ
    If once the day is lost.

Assured that few will follow me,
    And certain of defeat,
I am the rogue of chivalry,
    The knave who cannot cheat.

Then toss the coin and let it spin;
    And fall it head or tail,
The double dealer stands to win;
    At worst he cannot fail.

Some have the credit of intent,
    And some the joy of basking;
But why with one world be content
    When both are for the asking?

## NOVEMBER 11

You know not what you say,
  You saw not what was done
In England's evil day
  Ere yet that day was won.

When thousands do and die,
  The plaint is ever thus,
The children's angry cry
  'The teeth on edge for us.'

Harsh is the taste; and yet
  By grinding at the mill
In dust and dirt and sweat
  You shall not foot the bill.

No recompense may sweeten,
  No hardship can repay
The sour vintage eaten
  In England's evil day.

## AN EASY GAME

When in gall you have dipped your pen,
When you have whet your tongue-tip, then
Say to yourself before you sting
'Finding fault is an easy thing.'

When you have marked your victim down,
When you have tracked him through the town,
Say to yourself e'er the dart be hurled
'Nothing is easier in the world.'

If with a gibe you care to win,
Ending there where the rest begin,
Don't put a feather in your cap.
Even the meanest cur can yap.

Many a vision fades away,
Nimble feet are clogged with clay,
Golden voices of youth are drowned,
All because fault is easily found.

## SYMPATHY

How mighty is the strength of love,
    How wondrously revealed,
The many hundred pin-pricks prove
    By single dew-drops healed.

## THE HERD

With eyes that saw but light and shade
   The creature groped about
And herded to his kind, afraid
   Of that which was without:

Till one by one, and here and there,
   They dared to stand alone,
And shunned and hated what they were,
   And differed from their own.

Alert and radiant, brave and clean,
   Appeared the separate man;
The wonder of the world was seen;
   The game of life began.

The wheel of time revolves. To-day
   They grope and group anew;
What others think and do and say,
   They say and think and do.

Again they herd like kine or deer;
   But now with clouded mind
They crowd upon themselves, in fear
   Themselves of their own kind.

## EPITAPHS

### A THIRST

He was so good, so true a friend,
I drowned him at our journey's end.
Most gently did I put him out,
Most sweetly, in a pot of stout.
It were unreasoned to complain,
For certës he shall rise again.

### A SYNDIC

No teacher I of boys or smaller fry;
No teacher I of teachers; no, not I.
Mine was the distant aim, the longer reach,
To teach men how to teach men how to teach.

### ON A PHILOSOPHER

He read what other men had read,
And said what other men had said,
And surely, now that he is dead,
The road he trod the rest will tread
And read the books that once he read
And say the things that once he said.

### A LOST OPPORTUNITY

The flying chance, the golden gleam,
The idle hand, the empty net.

The backward glance, the dead regret,
The dust, and stream of covering sand.

## RELATIVITY

This new scheme of Einstein's,
    I suppose it's all right—
Nothing without the other thing,
    No loose without tight.

No man can be clever
    Unless someone's a fool;
And even good behaviour
    Has no standard or rule.

If nobody else was wicked,
    I shouldn't be good;
I couldn't be better than others,
    Do what I would.

All things are comparative;
    We rise if others drop;
Unless the rest are inferior,
    None can be at the top.

The only thought that troubles me
    And sometimes makes me sad,
Is—Had I not been so blameless,
    Others wouldn't be bad.

## THE CRITIC

A test most certain Peters had:
What other people praised, was bad.

## RETROSPECT

Any fool can see
  What all the world should do;
I alone am he
  At any moment who
Discerns what anyone
Should recently have done.

Others look ahead;
  But I can see what was;
Surelier I tread
  And wiselier, because
Of past events I find
The shadow cast behind.

Many search the morrow
  For vintage turning sour;
Some the cup of sorrow
  Fill from the passing hour;
I suck out—a plainer way—
The vapid lees of yesterday.

## FAVETE LINGVIS

We mustn't abuse him. His record was good.
For though he did nothing, he did what he could.

## THE SPECIALIST

Deep down beneath the common ground
   I delve and pierce the way,
Descend in ever-narrowing round
   Through dust and stone and clay,
Probing alone the dark profound
   Below the orb of day.

The outer air, so long the cone,
   Is now a disc of light;
The vortex drawn in tighter zone
   Points at the heart of night;
The lonely mind on this alone
   Centres its inward sight.

The darkest truths are hidden; so
   I downward, inward press,
And 'ever more and more I know
   Of ever less and less',
And distantly and dimly grow
   To next to nothingness.

## THE SHORT CUT

You say I merely notify disgust
At books that deal with common filth and lust,
Without dissecting and defining. Well,
Isn't that *your* way with a nasty smell?

## THE REPEATER

Full many a time and loud enough
   If only a thing is said,
Full many there are will take the stuff
   At length as daily bread.

I utter my thought a hundred times,
   A thing quite easily done,
And soon a score of apes and mimes
   Reflect the thought of one.

And that which many mouths commend,
   Though tin it be and brass,
Will ring as sterling gold at end
   Because it came to pass.

And I, who merely wanted it
   And therefore thought it best,
On high among the Doctors sit,
   A Lord of Truth confessed.

## THE DEATH WARRANT

Three withered men in minutes three
Condemned to death a lordly tree
That, slow, had topped the ways of men
Through three times three score years and ten.

## POETA NASCITUR

Said Johnson 'When my spirit sings,
    I write without a thought
And float away on airy wings
    Before my feet are caught.'

'And I,' said Brown, 'I think and think
    Till I can think no more,
And then I dip my quill in ink
    And write, but not before.'

In either case they hold to scorn
    The offspring of the brain.
Johnson will have it still unborn,
    And Brown prefers it slain.

So from two seeming opposites
    One truth I seem to see,
That, if I didn't use my wits,
    A poet I might be.

## THE KINGFISHER

Along the silver ice is shot
The single sky-blue thread; and not
A moment more is given to sight
Of that celestial delight.

## TASTE

Hardly the mind of man shall shift
    Aside from common pantomime;
This way or that it floats adrift
    Upon the swinging tides of time.

No hands are his to loose or bind;
    He shall not shape his taste or creed
Or take no colour from his kind
    Or sow the flower or kill the weed.

That which his lips had praised aloud
    If living when his sire was born,
Now, standing in the later crowd,
    He views aghast with eyes of scorn.

If he adore the gods that are,
    Let him beware of holy pride
And rather thank his natal star
    He lives e'er yet those gods have died.

Whether he smash the priceless glass,
    Or scrape its fragments from the pit,
Depends on when he came to pass
    And where in earth his lamp was lit.

## AUGUST 4

How simple now to mock
At those whose straining hands
Averted not the shock
That stunned a hundred lands.

How simple now to lay
The murder at the door
Of those who could not stay
The striding steps of war.

How simple now to damn
The eyes that saw too late
The wolf upon the lamb,
The Fury at the gate.

And England's golden sons
Who cast their flower and pride
Athwart the flaming guns,
And held the front, and died—

To say that all was lost
Because upon that scene
They counted not the cost,
How simple, and how mean.

# THE BEASTS THAT PERISH

Behold the beastliness of man:
Bag and bottle and broken can:
He I'ld rather be Satan than.

Over the land his lust has slain
He leaves his scum and filthy stain,
A creature God devised in vain.

For him the roads are flayed and racked,
The streams defiled, the woodland hacked,
For him—this foul miscarried fact.

His hoggës eyen cannot read
The book of beauty. Speed on speed
He lays, to go from greed to greed.

Behold him, honoured and divine,
Not understanding so decline
As to be likened to the swine.

And I, who with the Cherubim
Should soar beyond the dark and dim,
Am only a specimen of him.

## WITH CARE

I am a very careful man;
Very slowly I form a plan;
Very slowly I probe and test.
Nothing is good except the best.

All the imperfect is impure;
Only the faultless shal¹ endure.
I, in quest of the perfect, peep
Over the fence before I leap.

Warily down the longest lane
I pick my steps with care and pain.
Time is everything. Who shall say
That Rome was built in a single day?

Sooner than slip an inch or two
In things my hands have found to do,
I'ld travel on to the setting sun
And gladly rest with nothing done.

## THE WIRE-PULLER

If I plot and I plan,
  It is all for the best;
The machine is the man,
  And to hell with the rest.

I had rather be clever
  At pulling the strings
Than harvest whatever
  The business brings.

Provided I handle
  The puppets that play,
For game or for candle
  I care not who pay.

So close am I set
  Till the action is ended,
I wholly forget
  What the author intended.

What to me is the sound
  Or the sense of the scene,
So that under the ground
  I work the machine?

His brain must be woolly
  Who thinks anyone
Without lever and pulley
  Gets anything done.

## HOMO CREANS

I am the great god Man;
  Created, I create;
I magnify what God began,
  And break the bounds of Fate.

All matter in my hand
  Is clay to mix and mould;
The rocks, I sift them as the sand;
  The tin I turn to gold.

My sharp intelligence
  This way and that I fling.
I look, and all is shape and sense;
  I think, and lo! the thing.

## JOURNALESE

I am the siren Journalese;
I sit and moan across the seas;
My words are stale as mouldered cheese,
  But somehow pleasing found;
And never a roaming privateer
But stays his ship and anchors near
To sicken his soul and sate his ear
  With that insipid sound.

Come hither, all that sail the main,
For great and glorious is your gain
If here you learn the trite and plain
  More plain and trite to say.
And fear you not my lifelessness,
My faded face and dowdy dress;
For satisfied and knowing less
  I send you on your way.

## PROGRESS

I am the kind
   And gentle ogress;
I lead the blind,
   And my name is Progress.

Trust me, my son,
   And take my hand.
Keep on the run
   While others stand.

Some turn back,
   And some aside;
Keep you the track
   With me for guide.

Be not afraid;
   Firmly reject
The retrograde
   And the circumspect.

Nought should fetter
   The forward will;
Anything's better
   Than standing still.

To the cliff's brink
   When we are come,
Don't stop to think,
   Tumble down plumb.

Hang the repressive!
   Death to the slow!
Be a Progressive!
   Over you go!

## AT CROUGHTON LODGE, 1902

I am the Jack in Office.
*Who put you there?*
Devil I care.
I am the Jack in Office.

I get things done.
*Who told you to?*
Someone. Not you.
I get things done.

I tie the tape.
*What do you bind?*
Never you mind.
I tie the tape.

I am the new broom.
*Sweeping up what?*
Rather, what not?
I am the new broom.

I am the Appropriate Authority.
*Where's your cocked hat?*
No need for that.
I am the Appropriate Authority.

I shall rise from the dead.
*How do you know?*
God told me so.
I shall rise from the dead.

## JARGON

I am Jargon the Giant. I
Rebuild old Babel to the sky.
Fee Fi Fo Fum. Hee-haw. Bow-wow.
Who is the Lord of Language now?

Had God consulted me, no need
Ever had been for the big stampede.
One tongue can make confusion good
Provided by none is it understood.

## EFFICIENCY

I am Efficiency;
Something to do I see;
I never let things be;
   I'm on the run
And on the spot;
I do it; what,
It matters not;
   I get it done.

Bright as a pin,
Pardon I win
For sordid sin
   And common crime
If carried out
Complete without
A hitch or doubt
   And up to time.

## THE PRIZE-GIVING

And now I would like to say to *you*,
Who have *not* won prizes, a word or two.

Don't suppose that on that account
In after life you will never mount.

The fellow who gets to the top—egad!
It isn't always the brainy lad.

In after life—I am sixty-six—
It's *character* that wins the tricks.

Many a man in the highest class
At school was voted rather an ass.

Even I was an idle kid,
And never a stroke of work I did.

Nobody into my head could ram
An ounce of learning; and here I am.

So don't despair; for there well may be
Among you some who resemble me.

## ESCAPE

Because my faith will not adhere
   To any party creed,
I will not hold my country dear,
   Nor help her in her need.

Because I can but disbelieve
   In some recorded word
His Church would have me to receive,
   I have denied the Lord.

And since they seem with fable blent—
   The apple and the Fall—
I scrap the elder testament,
   And own no God at all.

He reaches home who runs away;
   And thus is freedom won.
Most surely does the letter slay
   When spirit there is none.


## TO A FRIEND OF YOUTH

Too often and in vain the sage
Decants the wines of crusted age;
But here in cups of seasoned truth
You blend the fragrant grapes of youth.

And drinking of that generous bowl
A boy shall know of life the whole,
And, entering at the narrow gate,
Shall view his manhood clear and straight.

## THE CRACKED GLASS

For *X* the world is all awry;
He loathes the earth and damns the sky;
He ever was born, he wonders why.

His fellow creature stirs his spleen;
In making object so obscene
What ever about could God have been?

Nor only wronged by man is he,
But scandalised by house and tree;
Just where they are, how dare they be?

Himself is his distorted view;
When squints the soul, then all's askew;
Nothing can then be clear or true.

The crookëd mirror of the mind
Will break the lovely light and find
Nature and God and man unkind.


## REQVIESCAT

Here lies a liar;
    Soft! Wake him not.
Bramble and briar,
    Hedge well the spot.

News from below
    If he retrieve,
No one will know
    What to believe.

## APOPHORETA

*Toast-rack*

> I glitter here for guest or host;
> They who despoil me love me most.

*Milk-jug*

> The promised land of Palestine
> Ran with no sweeter streams than mine.

*Pocket-case*

> Your wealth—in safe you needn't lock it;
> The safest locker is your pocket.

*Bad boy's book*

> If you are bad, or even worse,
> Then read my cautionary verse.

*Sealing-wax*

> Burn me and stamp me with your ring;
> You shall be potent as a king.

*Clothes-brush*

> Unless there's neither speck nor spot
> Upon your coat, despise me not.

*Elastic bands*

> See with what gentle strength we bind;
> So be you strict and be you kind.

*Butter-dish*

> Common I am, and yet I hold
> The one more certain bribe than gold.

*Knife*

> Some knots you may unravel; but
> I advocate the cleaner cut.

*Bottle of wine*

> Crown me with fairest diadem,
> The queen of wines, Château d'Yquem.

## THE DESTROYERS

No Hurry and Too Late
Sat together upon a gate.

To Too Late said No Hurry
'No cause I see for fear or worry.'

'There's nought we can do, at any rate'
To No Hurry said Too Late.

And as they spake, the wind blew
The poison seed, and the fungus grew.

'I wasn't told', No Hurry cried;
'What did I say?' Too Late replied.

## THE FLAW

Oh yes, I confess he has merits in plenty,
And points in his favour a dozen or twenty.

He is dutiful, true, incorruptible, good,
And, I have to admit it, he does what he should.

A splendid defender of God and the Right,
He's prudent in counsel and valiant in fight.

He is gifted with swiftness of body and mind;
He is generous, affable, modest and kind.

His face has a grace, and his voice is melodious;
I only dislike him because he is odious.

## REFLECTION

Men cast their eyes on those who pass
    And see themselves alone;
The image in the moving glass
    They know not for their own;
And some behold the goose and ass,
    And some the sloth and drone.

But you——. Because your soul is white
    And as a garden sweet,
A radiant and a heavenly sight
    Is every friend you meet,
And circled by the Sons of Light
    You walk the sapphired street.

## TO THE FAMILY

### ASH WEDNESDAY, 1927

Where Newton dared, am I to be afraid?
How could I dwell with Newton's holy shade?
And if I may with little impropriety
Be of the Family *and* of the Society,
I warrant you shall find me nothing loth
To eat with either and to drink with both,
Twice happy now if thus you condescend
To name me as your own familiar friend.

## APOPHORETA

*Pencil with india-rubber*
> Two things are good without a doubt—
> To write a thing: to rub it out.

*Pot of gum*
> Though others fail you at the last,
> I am a friend that sticketh fast.

*Box of matches*
> Whatever valiant deeds are done,
> *We* are a match for *anyone*.

*Shaving-soap*
> No real risk you'll run with me,
> However close your shaves may be.

*Two-foot rule*
> Greeting, good sir. We both are straight,
> Two-footed, just and accurate.

*Penknife*
> When all debate is out of joint,
> Depend on me to make a point.

*Egg-cup*
> I serve an end; for even an egg
> On which to stand must have a leg.

*Studs*
> In every race, it seems to me,
> The stud will show the pedigree.

*Ball of string*
> In county courts or courts of kings
> Without me no one pulls the strings.

## THE SHOWN HAND

Says Antony 'In politics
    I keep my outlook wide;
Freely with these and those I mix,
    And take not either side',

And, talking, waxes eloquent
    And lifts his voice on high
Unto whatever parliament
    There chances to be nigh.

A clerk of old (I've read in Greek)
    Thus wrote unto a friend:
'The sample of my hand you seek
    I have no mind to send.'

# ENGLAND

I

Do you see the beauty
  Of your native land?
Then it is your duty
  Not so still to stand,
Not so long to linger
  Touched with no dismay,
Lifting not a finger,
  Till it pass away.

Bred in smothered city
  If you sightless live,
Then for very pity
  None will not forgive.
Do you truly mean it?
  Do you mean it not?
Never to have seen it—
  Ah the cruel lot!

Many without reason
  Look on land and sky,
See the various season,
  Like the beasts that die—
See the sun and shadow
  Blue and grey and green,
Wood and stream and meadow—
  See, and have not seen.

# ENGLAND

## II

Green England, loveliest living
    Of all the lands on earth—
God hear my high thanksgiving
    That England gave me birth:
Warm land of golden meadows
    And cold with splendid dews,
That ever springs and runs and sings
    With Usk and Esk and Ouse.

Mine are the hues unnumbered,
    The distant faded down,
The nearer upland umbered
    With clustered forest brown;
The black tilth of the fenland,
    The plains that shade and shine,
The glimmering sand, the twilit land,
    The clouded seas are mine.

Nowhere so kindly stealing,
    Nowhere with softer change
The coloured year goes wheeling
    About the barn and grange—
The gray frost, and the glory
    Of April's white attire,
And roseate days of heat and haze,
    And autumn fledged with fire.

Behold, my soul, the showers
    Of silver rain, behold
The woodland blue with flowers,
    The meadow strown with gold,
The willowed wandering waters,
    The scarlet beechen floor,
The towered elm in dusky realm,
    Behold them, and adore.

## THEORY

Of frothy stuff
And windy word,
Good sir, I've heard
    Enough.

Name me an act,
Something done
Full in the sun,
    A fact.

In overmuch
You give me not
A single spot
    To touch.

With head in mist
You do not know
What things below
    Exist.

And what you mean,
My worthy man,
I simply can-
    not glean.

## DISCONTENT

To mumble and to grumble
  Is slippery sin;
  And when we begin,
We stumble and we tumble
  Headlong in.
Learn, O Man, to be humble,
  And kind to your kin.

## UNCERTAINTY

On rocking land
  And heaving sea
How hard to stand
  For you and me.

To whom to hearken,
  Which way to go,
In days that darken
  How hard to know.

## ESPRIT D'ESCALIER

If only, John, before I went
From yesternight's hot argument,
Not mastered and yet ill-content—

If only I'd remembered there
The point that met me on the stair,
Clean and sharp in the outer air—

Before that devastating thrust
Your stubborn front, I'll wager, must
Have cracked, and crumbled into dust;

And crumpled up, you dear old John,
To bed you would at last have gone
With not a leg to stand upon.

I turned to take the field once more
And lay you fairly on the floor.
Why had you locked, so soon, the door?

## THE JUG AND THE MUG

The Jug
Said to the Mug
'You
Have nothing to do,
Not even to think.
Stand still
While I
Give you your fill.
From you
The shallow and dry
Will drink.'

## ON A PSYCHOLOGIST

Here lies a Student of the Mind
  Who toiled with zest unblunted;
He played himself at hoodman-blind,
  The hunter and the hunted.

The truth about himself he sought,
  And mightily he sought it;
He ever thought of what he thought
  And why he thought he thought it.

Within himself from early youth,
  Although he never found it,
He sought about himself the truth,
  And now is buried round it.

## PEGASUS

Whoso has caught the fleet wild sound,
  And bridled it with sense,
Shall scour the fathomless profound
  And measure the immense.

Music untamed, though swift and strong,
  Shall prove of fading worth;
And sense, without the wings of song,
  Must walk the roads of earth.

## THE RIGHT MAN

Where it is due, right gladly
  I give the credit.
It wanted saying badly,
  And Judson said it.

## THE FIVE FALLIBLES

Some folk are disgustingly clever,
    And some are delightfully dense.
I prefer to be seen betwixt and between,
    And to talk to the people of sense.

The senses are fallible.  Granted:
    I've read it in many a book.
Yet I think it as well to taste and to smell,
    To touch and to listen and look.


## CULTURE

    The Popinjay or Pee Wee
    May say his say in Soho
    Or Mandalay or Hong Kong.

    Here if thou'lt be a Big Wig,
    See that thou flee from Clap Trap,
    Bow not the knee to Hum Drum.

    Take not thy kit from Rag-Bag,
    Tune not thy wit to Dead Head,
    Here if thou'lt sit with Big Wig.

    To top of tree who fly high
    With Litt.D. should hob nob
    And men like me and Big Wig.

## DRIED

I am the dry stick,
   I am the bare bone;
Sooner shall you lick
   Blood from a stone,

Sooner make simmer
   The Arctic Sea,
Than get you one glimmer
   Out of me.

## VITIOSA CVRA

Far from my telephone,
   Far from my friends and sins,
Out in the central sea, alone
   I lie, and the Band begins.

In vain the first-class fare,
   And cabin of a lord:
Unseen with me from God knows where
   The Jazz-Band stepped on board.

From evils we deplore
   We may not safely flee;
Man's empire stops not with the shore,
   But stains the sacred sea.

## NEFANDA

O sir, in this celestial clime,
Where every moment is sublime,
I have no will to squander time.

To learn elsewhere might please me much
What views are held by such and such
Of those with whom you live in touch,

Or what your children cost in fees,
Or why you gave up keeping bees,
Or what it is that makes us sneeze.

But here, with changing sky, I find
I change my mood if not my mind,
And certain things I leave behind.


## A POSTERIORE

That woman who waddles in trousers tight
Can never have viewed her hinder sight
Or learnt that disguise is the true escape
From certain flaws in the female shape,
And that dress was intended, loose or close,
To adorn the graceful and hide the gross.

## THE HOLY SEPULCHRE

A point on earth's enormous face,
Whirled with her motions into space,
The magnet of the ransomed race;

By fanatic and fratricide
Drowned, and resurgent in the tide
Of conquest; scorned and glorified;

Hammered and hacked and fired and wrecked,
Anon by victor architect
In reverence and beauty decked;

The goal of angered ardent eyes,
The badge of battle, and the prize
Of all the mailëd chivalries:

Stubborn and still, through flame and sword,
Here, for its emptiness adored,
Sticks fast the trophy of the Lord.

## CARMEL

Across the wide and sleeping blue
The Land of Promise sinks from view,
And Carmel Mount, that towered high,
Fades and falls in the far grey sky.

And now all dim, and drowned in dream,
Across the Sea of Ages seem
The altar and the awful seer,
The eyes amazed with fire and fear.

## A CREED

My son, God made thee one in three
   Of head and hand and heart;
Now see that in this trinity
   Each person plays its part.

Alone the head is monstrous grown
   And prematurely old;
Alone the hand is stiff as stone;
   Alone the heart is cold.

Coequal are the vital three,
   And none is more or less;
The three in one and one in three,
   My son, thou shalt confess.

Its golden mist the willow lights
   While yet we only dream
Of what shall fall from azure heights
   On shore and stream.

And when the woods are grey and bare,
   And dark the waters pass,
Faithful it hangs its amber hair
   Over the glass.

The eyes that earliest read the book
   Of Beauty, read it late,
And back with fond remembrance look,
   And, hopeful, wait.

For EU product safety concerns, contact us at Calle de José Abascal, 56–1°, 28003 Madrid, Spain or eugpsr@cambridge.org.